P9-APJ-832

GREEN-
COLLAR
CAREERS

BUILDING GREEN PLACES

CAREERS IN PLANNING, DESIGNING, AND BUILDING

By Ruth Owen

CRABTREE
Publishing Company
www.crabtreebooks.com

Crabtree Publishing Company

Author: Ruth Owen
Publishing plan research and development:
   Sean Charlebois, Reagan Miller
   Crabtree Publishing Company
Editors: Mark Sachner, Molly Aloian
Proofreader: Reagan Miller, Ellen Rodger
Editorial director: Kathy Middleton
Photo research: Ruth Owen
Designer: Westgrapix/Tammy West
Production coordinator: Margaret Amy Salter
Prepress technician: Samara Parent
Production: Kim Richardson
Curriculum adviser: Suzy Gazlay, M.A.
Editorial consultant: James Marten, Ph.D.; Chair, Department
   of History, Marquette University, Milwaukee, Wisconsin

Written, developed, and produced by Water Buffalo Books

Photographs and reproductions
Alamy: David J. Green: page 13 (bottom); Lee Beel: page 14 (top); Jeff Morgan,
   Alternative Technology: page 18 (top); Camera Lucida: page 18 (bottom
   left); Adrian Sherratt: page 18 (bottom right); Les Ladbury: page 20
   (bottom); page 26; Jim West: page 39 (right); Axel Leschinski: page 47 (left);
   Axel Leschinski: page 47 (right); Clynt Garnham: page 50; Ros Drinkwater:
   page 52; Paul Glendell: page 54; page 55 (bottom)
Marilyn Brownlee: page 40
Corbis: Ariel Skelley: page 1 (center); Tim Pannell: page 25 (bottom right); Ariel
   Skelley: page 29; page 31 (bottom); page 36 (right); Heino Kalis: page 41
   (left); Michael Boys: page 45; Alessia Pierdomenico: page 53 (bottom)
Tom Deininger: page 35
Dockside Green: page 10 (bottom left); page 10 (bottom right); page 48. Forest
   Stewardship Council (Eric Goethals): page 17 (all)
La Rosa Campsite: page 58 (bottom)
Luis de Garrido: page 16 (top)
Getty Images: Ahmad Zamroni: page 15 (bottom); Robert Nickelsberg: pages
   22-23 (background)
Jeremy Levine Design: page 27 (bottom all)
Rachael Morton, Associates III: page 36 (left)
Natural Insulations: page 23 (right)
NYC Garbage Cube: page 37 (bottom)
Retrouvius: page 21 (all)
ROEWU Architecture: page 19
Ruby Tuesday Books Ltd: page 11 (top); page 41 (right); page 42 (top center);
   page 42 (top right).
Shutterstock: page 1 (top all); pages 4-5 (all); page 6 (all); page 7; page 8 (all);
   page 9; page 10 (top); page 11 (bottom); page 12; page 13 (top left); page 13
   (top right); page 13 (center left); page 13 (center right); page 14 (bottom);
   page 15 (top); page 15 (top inset); page 16 (bottom); page 23 (center); page 25
   (top); page 25 (bottom left); page 27 (top); page 27 all; pages 32-33 (all); page
   38 (left top); page 38 (left center); page 38 (left bottom); page 42 (left); page
   43 (all); page 46; page 49; page 53 (top);
   page 58 (top).
Studio Arihiro Miyake: page 37 (center). Superstock: pages 38-39 (background)
VAHO: page 37 (top right); page 37 (top left)
Vincent Callebaut Architecture—www.vincent.callebaut.org: page 51
White House Photograph (Joyce N. Boghosian): page 44
The WILD Center (Tupper Lake): page 31 (top)
Wikipedia (public domain): page 20 (top); page 30 (all); page 34; page 55 (top);
   page 55 (center); page 56; page 57

Library and Archives Canada Cataloguing in Publication

Available at Library and Archives Canada

Library of Congress Cataloging-in-Publication Data

Owen, Ruth, 1967-
  Building green places : careers in planning, designing, and building /
Ruth Owen.
    p. cm. -- (Green-collar careers)
  Includes index.
  ISBN 978-0-7787-4863-2 (pbk. : alk. paper) -- ISBN 978-0-7787-4852-6
(reinforced library binding : alk. paper)
  1. Sustainable design--Vocational guidance--Juvenile literature. I. Title.
II. Series.

NK1520.O94 2009
720'.47--dc22

2009028072

Crabtree Publishing Company

www.crabtreebooks.com   1-800-387-7650
Copyright © **2010 CRABTREE PUBLISHING COMPANY**. All rights reserved. No part of this publication may be reproduced, stored in a retrieval
system or be transmitted in any form or by any means, electronic, mechanical, photocopying, recording, or otherwise, without the prior written
permission of Crabtree Publishing Company.

**Published
in Canada
Crabtree Publishing**
616 Welland Ave.
St. Catharines, Ontario
L2M 5V6

**Published in
the United States
Crabtree Publishing**
PMB16A
350 Fifth Ave., Suite 3308
New York, NY 10118

**Published in the
United Kingdom
Crabtree Publishing**
Maritime House
Basin Road North, Hove
BN41 1WR

**Published
in Australia
Crabtree Publishing**
386 Mt. Alexander Rd.
Ascot Vale (Melbourne)
VIC 3032

CONTENTS

R0431093739

BUILDING A GREEN FUTURE

Plumber

Carpenter

Gardener

You wake up. It's a hot, sunny morning, but you don't need to turn on the air-conditioning. This is because the house has walls made from straw that keep your home cool in summer and warm in winter.

After a shower—using water heated by the Sun—you pick some organic strawberries and peaches from your balcony for breakfast.

With breakfast over, you check your emails while the biodigester machine in your basement turns your breakfast scraps into electricity to power your laptop.

When it's time for work, you set off on your bicycle along the City Cycleway. The wide, safe, cycles-only roadway can easily be reached from every house and apartment in the city. The cycleway takes you through the city's Zero Carbon Forest—a wide expanse of trees around the city that helps remove damaging greenhouse gases from the air.

Growing our own food cuts down on the need to transport produce. Even the smallest space, such as a balcony (near right) can be used to grow organic vegetables and fruit.

Trees naturally absorb carbon dioxide from the air (far right). Therefore, planting trees is a good way for a city to try to lower, or even eliminate, its carbon emissions.

Green Archite...
Eco-Designe...
Solar Panel Insta...

You emerge from the trees and pedal across a wildflower meadow, where the giant wind turbines that power the city are hard at work making electricity.

Once at your desk, you enjoy the view from your office's window wall. As you work you look out over a beautiful lake where birds are swimming and people are waterskiing and wind surfing. Once upon a time this space was a giant, ugly hole in the ground where limestone was quarried for use in construction....

CAREER PROFILE

WORKING WITH GREEN ENERGY: SOLAR PANEL INSTALLER

I always knew that I wanted to do something to do with the environment. I also knew that I didn't want a desk job! I was interested in solar power, so I took a week-long course and learned the theory behind using solar panels and how to install them. Now I work as part of a small crew installing solar panels.

An average day at the start of a new job begins with loading the truck. When we get to the job, there are ladders to be set up and equipment to be carried up onto the roof. The job combines physical work—climbing and lifting—with the technical work of setting up the panels and connecting them into the electrical system of the house.

I love being outside in nature—there's nothing like hearing coyotes howling as you pack up your tools at the end of a long day!

This is a fast-moving new industry, so most people are learning on the job. It's worth taking some courses, though, in electrics or renewable energy.

**Kristin Underwood
Solar panel installer
California**

Wind power is created using wind turbines. The wind spins the turbine's blades (far left), turning a copper coil inside a magnetic field. This creates an electrical current that is fed into the main electricity grid of an area.

Cycling (left) is good for our health and a clean, green way to travel.

WHAT IS CLIMATE CHANGE?

Climate change is the gradual increase in temperatures that our planet is experiencing. Today, most scientists agree that this increase is caused by humans burning fossil fuels, such as oil and coal. Burning fossil fuels releases harmful gases, such as carbon dioxide, methane, and nitrous oxide, into the atmosphere. These gases have become known as "greenhouse gases."
This is because they are trapping heat from the Sun on Earth in the way that the glass of a greenhouse traps heat inside. Our planet needs heat and light from the Sun in order for life to flourish on Earth, but too much heat is a bad thing. Parts of the world will become too dry for food to grow. Our weather will become more extreme, causing hurricanes, heat waves, and torrential rain. Glaciers and the giant "caps" of ice at the north and south poles will melt. This will cause ocean levels to rise.

Cement is made from limestone. This rock must be dug from quarries. The creation of quarries damages the landscape, destroys natural habitats, and creates dust and noise.

Some scientists predict that if all the ice in Earth's glaciers melted, ocean levels would rise by over 200 feet (60 meters). Low-lying cities, such as New York and London, would disappear under water!

Working For A Greener Future

For those of us who care about our planet and want to live a greener life, this would be our ideal way to live. Unfortunately, our buildings and cities are not that green—yet. All these "green" ways of living and working are available to us today, however. It's just that not everyone has heard about them—and that's where you come in!

Earth in Crisis

Our planet is facing many challenges for the future. One of these is climate change caused by the release of greenhouse gases, such as carbon dioxide, methane, and nitrous oxide, into the atmosphere. Another is pollution and the problem of what to do with all the garbage we produce. We also need to figure out how to save energy that comes from fossil fuels that are running out, such as coal and oil.

We must also develop ways of using more energy from sources that are renewable, such as wind power and solar power, which will not run out.

These challenges affect the way we use energy in just about everything we do. The way we construct our buildings, and the way we use them, plays a big part in causing problems such as climate change, pollution, and the overuse of non-renewable materials and fossil fuels.

Construction: Greenhouse Gases and Energy Use

The manufacture of building materials, such as steel and cement, uses huge quantities of energy. It also releases vast amounts of greenhouse gases into the atmosphere. Transporting those materials also burns oil.

Every time we burn fossil fuels—for example, gasoline in a truck or coal to make electricity—the greenhouse gas carbon dioxide, CO_2, is released into the air. The release of carbon dioxide is known as "carbon emissions."

"Our planet is in peril. The main culprit: greenhouse-gas emissions that are turning the Earth into an oven. ... America emits more greenhouse gasses than any other country. ... Our buildings account for more of our greenhouse-gas emissions—a whopping 40 percent—than anything else, including transportation."

Van Jones,
Special adviser on green jobs
to the Obama administration

Large amounts of oil and electricity are used to power equipment and tools on construction sites.

WHAT IS A CARBON FOOTPRINT?

A carbon footprint is the measure of how much carbon dioxide, CO_2, something is responsible for. Each person on Earth has a carbon footprint. Every time you take a car ride or watch TV, your activities are producing CO_2 that is added to your carbon footprint. An average person living in North America is responsible for approximately 20 tons of CO_2 each year. An average person living in a poorer country, such as India, produces less than 2,000 pounds (900 kilograms) of CO_2 in a year. To halt climate change, people in wealthier countries must decrease the size of their carbon footprints.

It's not just people who have carbon footprints; buildings do, too. Every CO_2-producing activity in the construction of a building or in its eventual use adds to a building's carbon footprint.

Measuring carbon emissions is one way to find out how damaging to the environment something is. We call these measurements a "carbon footprint."

Construction: Pollution and Waste

Construction sites can cause a lot of pollution. Fumes from paints, glues, and other chemical-based substances pollute the air. Dust from concrete, cement, wood, and stone can be blown for many miles. So, too, can the smoke from construction-site bonfires.

It's not just the air that's affected by construction pollution. Oil, toxic paints, glues, cleaning products, and construction dust and garbage can all find their way into local ponds and rivers.

Like every other building, the skyscraper shown here has a carbon footprint. Both of the photos to the right show the use of energy in the construction of a building like this. They show how energy is used to manufacture the building's steel frame. Oil is used to power the cranes that put up the building and the machines that turn iron into steel. Once the building is in use, electricity will be used to light and heat the building and power the elevators. All these activities create carbon emissions.

These substances can destroy wild habitats and kill fish, birds, and other animals. The pollution can be washed into waterways when it rains or soak into the ground and pollute the groundwater. Groundwater collects and runs below the surface of the land. It eventually flows into streams and rivers and is an important part of our overall water supply on Earth.

Each year, billions of tons of waste from construction projects are dumped in landfills (garbage dumps where the waste is simply buried underground). Some of the waste is toxic, and much of it is not biodegradable, so it will not decompose, or rot away. Waste such as metals and plastics will simply lie in the ground for hundreds, or even thousands, of years.

UNHEALTHY BUILDINGS

The way we construct our buildings has not just been bad for the environment; it's also bad for our health! We rely on air-conditioning systems that circulate cool but stale air instead of installing systems that carry fresh air in and out of our homes. Paints, varnishes, furniture, and carpets made from chemical-based, plastic, or other synthetic substances give off toxic fumes that cause allergies, asthma, headaches, and other health problems. Tomorrow's green buildings must use more natural materials, bring fresh air and sunlight into our lives, and banish chemicals that cause sickness from our buildings.

A huge amount of construction waste is actually made up of new materials that were simply not needed. A study in the United Kingdom showed that 13 million tons of brand new construction materials end up in UK landfills each year—just because construction companies order too much!

Gardeners pour gallons of water onto grass lawns and water-hungry plants in areas where the climate is dry and hot and better suited to desert-like plants. A lawn sprinkler can use as much water in one hour as a family of four uses in a whole day!

"If everyone in the world lived like the average North American we would need five planets to live on."

One Planet Living Initiative

Environmentally Unfriendly Buildings

It's not just the building materials and construction methods that make our homes, schools, offices, and other buildings unfriendly to our planet. How we use our buildings can be damaging, too.

Many of our buildings are not energy efficient. This means they use more energy than is really needed to light them, heat them, and operate appliances and machines. They also use electricity from coal-burning power plants and oil-burning heating systems.

The amount of water we waste is also an important issue to think about. Most of our buildings and gardens have not been designed to be water-wise. We waste water by using showers, toilets, dishwashers, and washing machines that use more water than is needed to do their jobs.

If we want to protect our planet for the future, green construction and green buildings are essential.

Dockside Green is a planned carbon-neutral community in Victoria, British Columbia, Canada. Every home will be fitted with a carbon monitor that allows residents to measure the amount of energy and water they are using.

The Future of Construction

Governments around the world are putting new laws in place to ensure that new buildings are water and energy efficient and are constructed using environmentally friendly materials and building methods. Green designers and construction companies are finding ways to reduce, recycle, and reuse. They use construction materials, such as wood, and even straw, that are renewable and do not use a lot of energy in their production. They design innovative ways for their buildings to use less electricity and water. Many builders use recycled products—for example, insulation material (which keeps buildings cool in summer and warm in winter) that is made from old newspapers or recycled denim.

Tomorrow's Construction Workers

Without a doubt, the drive to make construction greener is now underway. Finding new ways to do something can be very rewarding. You must be creative and innovative. You need to think like an inventor and be ready to experiment. The construction industry needs people like this for the future. Worldwide, the construction industry employs millions of people—from architects who design new buildings, to construction workers who build them. If you like the idea of creating beautiful, green buildings that are good for our planet, a career in the green construction industry could be for you!

Many builders reuse bricks, stone, wood, tiles, windows, doors, lights, and other materials and items from old buildings that have been demolished. Reusing old materials means they aren't dumped in landfills. Reclamation, or salvage, companies (as above) sell these materials.

There are many different roles to be filled in the creation of green buildings: from interior designers who come up with new ideas for using furniture, to manufacturers of the products themselves; from scientists who develop eco-friendly paints, to artists who decorate new public buildings with eco-friendly amazing murals.

BUILDING MATERIALS— GREEN OR NOT SO GREEN?

Some building materials are greener than others. Green construction takes into account a lot of factors: How renewable is a material? What level of carbon emissions did its production and transportation create? Can it be reused or recycled if the building is demolished in the future? Is waste from the material biodegradable? When combined with other materials, how efficient will it be at keeping a building cool in summer and warm in winter?

Many architects design buildings made from locally quarried stone. This cuts down on carbon emissions from transportation and means the building has been created using a local resource.

All of these factors are important in determining whether or not a material has good "green" possibilities. Most materials, if used the right way, can be helpful in constructing buildings that are clean, energy efficient, and environmentally friendly.

Rock

Rock is a completely natural material. It is used to build walls and to make floor tiles and kitchen surfaces. There are vast quantities of rock on Earth, but it has to be dug from the ground or from a cliff or mountain in a place known as a quarry. The creation of a quarry damages a large area of land. Quarrying rocks, cutting and shaping them, and delivering them to construction sites uses energy and produces carbon emissions.

Stone walls can be very energy efficient, though. They can keep a building cool, but some types of stone also soak up heat during the day and then release it into the building when the outside temperature cools.

HOW IS A BUILDING CONSTRUCTED?

Buildings can be constructed in a lot of different ways.

Apartment blocks and commercial buildings (offices, stores, and factories) usually have a framework made from steel.

Panels of metal, concrete, or glass cover the frame. Sometimes bricks are used on the outside of the building.

Houses are normally built with a frame made of wood.

The outside of the building is then covered with a weatherproof material such as brick, stone, stucco, or wood or vinyl siding.

Houses can also be built from concrete blocks that are then covered with stone or stucco.

Inside the building, drywall (plasterboard) sheets are attached to the framework. Sometimes the sheets are covered with a smooth layer of plaster that can be painted or have wallpaper glued to it.

The Messingham nature reserve in Lincolnshire, UK, was once a sand quarry. Today, the lagoons created by sand excavation, and the surrounding countryside, are home to 370 plant species and 180 species of birds.

When they are no longer in use, quarries can be turned into nature reserves. Large pits can be flooded with water to create a water habitat, and wild plants and animals soon take over bare, rocky landscape.

Rock is as hard as—well, rock! This means it is tough and can be reused again and again.

Concrete

Concrete is a hard, strong material that is used in many different ways to strengthen buildings. It is also used to make the foundations (the base) of buildings and to make concrete blocks. Concrete is an important construction material, but it is very damaging to the environment. Some scientific studies have shown that concrete is responsible for five percent of the world's carbon emissions!

Concrete is made from cement mixed with sand, water, and ground-up rock, such as gravel. The main environmental problem with concrete is one of its ingredients—cement. Cement binds all the other ingredients of concrete together and makes them set rock hard. The problem is that cement is manufactured by heating limestone rock to around 2,600 degrees Fahrenheit (1,427 degrees Celsius). The "cooked" limestone is then ground into a powder. This process uses massive quantities of energy and produces large amounts of carbon emissions.

Building with concrete uses vast quantities of water to make the concrete mix—in fact, thousands of gallons of water are needed to make enough concrete for just one house! Here, a construction worker uses concrete to lay a base for a house.

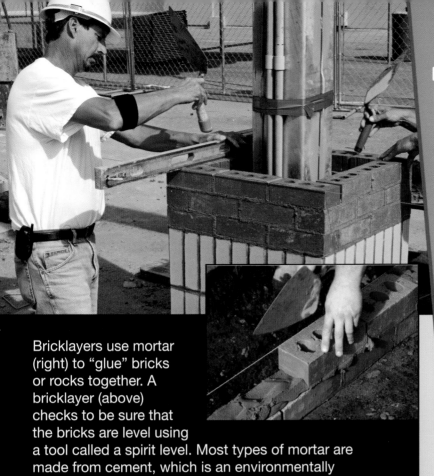

Bricklayers use mortar (right) to "glue" bricks or rocks together. A bricklayer (above) checks to be sure that the bricks are level using a tool called a spirit level. Most types of mortar are made from cement, which is an environmentally unfriendly material.

INTRODUCING COW DUNG BRICKS!

In Indonesia, a group of green-thinking young business people have started a company, EcoFaeBrick, that makes bricks from cow dung! The bricks are strong, clean, healthy to use, and very good for the environment. Cow dung is a highly renewable resource—in fact, farmers end up with too much of it—whereas the excavation of clay to make bricks destroys large areas of land that would be better used for growing food. In addition to using the dung as the main ingredient in the bricks themselves, the bricks are fired (baked) using bio gas as the energy source. The bio gas is made from methane released by cow dung.

Bricks

Bricks are usually made from clay, a material that appears naturally on Earth. The clay is gathered from the bottom of large lakes or from clay pits that are similar to quarries. At a brickworks, the clay is mixed with water, poured into a mold, and baked at over 2,000 degrees Fahrenheit (1,093 degrees Celsius). This uses a lot of energy and creates carbon emissions. Bricks then have to be transported from the brickworks to construction sites.

When an old brick building is demolished, the bricks can be reused in a new building. Also, to make bricks more eco-friendly, some brick manufacturers are now using recycled glass and other recycled materials in the brick mixture. This stops these materials from going into landfills, and it helps the bricks fire (bake) at lower temperatures.

Selling their unwanted cow dung provides farmers (like this dairy farmer) with additional income.

15

THE R4 HOUSE

The R4 House was designed by Italian architect Luis de Garrido. The house was constructed using six steel shipping containers. No waste materials were created in the building of the house, and it can be demolished and the components reused in the future. The R4 house has a green roof made of plants that helps insulate the house and creates a natural habitat for wildlife. The four Rs in the name stand for Reuse, Recuperate (reclaim), Recycle, and Reasoning—thinking about how to change the way we construct our buildings.

Above: a computer-generated illustration of the R4 House.

Right: Shipping containers, like those shown here, are giant steel boxes used for transporting goods on cargo ships. There are thousands of unused shipping containers around the world doing nothing but littering industrial areas and dockyards. Now, green designers are using them to create homes, offices, and even hotels!

Steel

Steel is a material made from iron ore mixed with coke (a material made from coal), limestone, and small quantities of other metals. To make new steel, iron must be mined and then processed using huge amounts of energy and water. Although the steel-making process also produces large quantities of carbon emissions, steel is 100 percent recyclable. Making one ton of new recycled steel from old steel items saves 2,500 pounds (1,133 kg) of iron ore, 1,400 pounds (635 kg) of coal, and 120 pounds (54 kg) of limestone! Recycling steel also uses less energy than making new steel, and it keeps the old items made out of steel from ending up in landfills. Sometimes pieces of steel can be taken from an old building and reused in a new project.

Wood

Wood is a natural material that is 100 percent renewable, but it should only be used from sustainable sources, such as FSC certified forests, forests that have

been planted for the lumber industry, or from old trees that need to be cut down to maintain the health of a natural forest. Wood should never be used from endangered habitats, such as tropical rain forests.

Trees simply need to be cut down, cut to size, and then delivered to the construction site as lumber. If you took a quantity of wood and a quantity of newly made steel, making the steel would use 140 percent more energy and create 45 percent more carbon emissions than processing the wood. Wood from an old building can be reused in its current form, or reshaped, and if wood ends up in a landfill, it is completely biodegradable. Wood has good insulation properties, too.

During the life of a lumber forest it becomes a habitat for thousands of birds, insects, and other animals.

LOOK FOR THE FSC MARK

The Forest Stewardship Council (FSC) is an international, non-governmental organization founded to protect the world's forests and to ensure they are used in a sustainable way. This is what the FSC logo means:

• The wood has come from a forest in which the trees are replaced or allowed to regenerate.

• The forestry company employs local people and respects their rights to live in and use the forest.

• Endangered animals and plants in the forest are protected.

Lumber, flooring, and furniture companies that use FSC wood display the logo (shown below) on their products.

At this tree nursery in Mexico, trees are grown to restock FSC-certified forests.

Straw

Yes—that scratchy yellow stuff that horses have in their stables! Remember how we said green construction is all about invention and experimentation? Building a house from straw bales is very eco-friendly and becoming very popular. Straw is the leftover stalks from food crops such as wheat, oats, and rice. The straw is simply dried and packed into bales on a farm. Straw buildings are constructed using the bales like giant bricks. The bales are held together by wire and the building is then covered with stucco and plaster. The walls are very thick, so they are super-insulated!

Construction workers fit wooden window frames into the straw walls of a straw bale house. A straw bale can cost just a few dollars, and about 500 bales are enough to build a family-sized house.

The outside walls of this straw house (below left) have been covered with stucco. Inside, a straw bale house (right) looks just like any other house!

Bamboo

Bamboo is an evergreen grass that is grown in Southeast Asia, and parts of Australia and the southwestern United States. There are 1,000 different species of bamboo, and some have thick, strong stems that can actually be used in construction. Some construction companies in dry, warm areas are using bamboo to build the framework of houses. Bamboo can also be used to make flooring, walls, and furniture. Bamboo is a 100 percent renewable resource and is completely biodegradable. Some species of bamboo can grow over one foot (30 centimeters) in a day!

Bamboo is not grown all over the world, so it sometimes has to be transported very long distances. This uses energy and produces carbon emissions.

CAREER PROFILE

BUILDING WITH STRAW AND MUD!: ECO-FRIENDLY BUILDER

When I first started out on my own, I was lucky to be put in touch with a couple who wanted to build a straw bale house. I took a week-long course on straw bale building and then helped them create a design and plans for the house. It was a great learning experience, and now I use their house as a "show home" to promote my company.

So far, I've built two straw bale houses and a passive solar house (a house that uses only the Sun's energy for heating and lighting). We used adobe as the main construction material because it holds the Sun's heat really well and then releases it into the house at night when the air cools.

I'm on site most days when there's a project underway. I do the hands-on building, find other green contractors to work with me, go out in the truck to buy materials—everything!

Nathan Land
Contractor
H & P Design / Build
Hartford, Connecticut

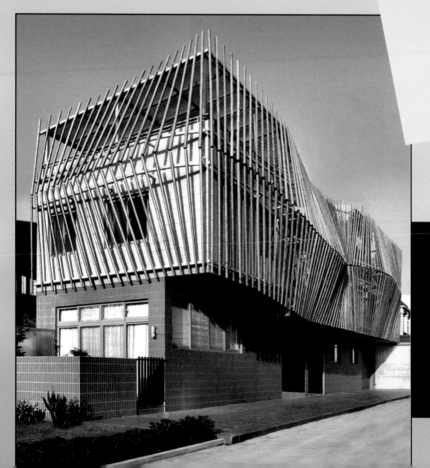

This innovative bamboo design was created by ROEWU Architecture for this house in Taiwan. The bamboo screen around the house offers security (instead of using metal window bars) and allows fresh air to enter the windows and open areas (at the top of the building) instead of using air conditioning.

EARTHSHIPS

"Earthships" came from the imagination of eco-architect Michael Reynolds. Earthships are completely self-sufficient homes. They obtain all their water by harvesting rainwater, and they use solar and wind power. Earthships are built from used tires filled with soil then stacked like bricks. The whole structure is covered with clay or adobe, and one side of the building is banked into the earth to help insulate the house. The original Earthships were built in Taos, New Mexico, in the late 1980s. Today, there are Earthships in other parts of the United States, the United Kingdom, Spain, France, and even Siberia.

An Earthship can use up hundreds, or even thousands, of tires (right) that would otherwise have ended up in landfills. Bottles and cans are also used to make the walls. The bases of glass bottles can be seen in the walls of the Earthship shown above.

Adobe

Adobe has been used to build homes for thousands of years! Adobe is a mixture of clay, sand, water, and straw. The mixture is poured into a brick-shaped mold and left to dry naturally in the Sun. Adobe can also be smoothed over walls and used like stucco. It is a completely natural material and is normally made using locally available materials. It is therefore very eco-friendly and is very efficient at insulating a building.

Demolition to Design

Green designers and builders often use reclaimed materials. Reclaimed materials have an almost zero impact on the environment because the energy used to make new materials is saved. Reclaiming materials also cuts down on the amount of landfill needed.

Reclamation companies deconstruct (take apart) buildings that are due for demolition, or are being refitted, and then sell the items at a reclamation yard or store.

If you like the idea of recycling and making money from something that someone else thought was junk, a career in reclamation could be for you!

CAREER PROFILE

SECOND TIME AROUND: RECLAMATION DEALER

No careers adviser ever mentioned that there was such a career as reclamation, but when I realized that selling stuff other people didn't want was a good way to earn a living—that was it!

While I was doing my architect's degree, I bought a small flat (apartment) that needed lots of restoration. I needed to repair and restore the flat on a zero budget so I was finding the materials I needed on demolition sites and in dumpsters. That's how I got started.

Now I buy and sell architectural salvage for a living. I've made lots of contacts with demolition companies. They let me know when they find something interesting or when they are going to be stripping out a building. I visit the site and check out any useful items or materials. I also buy items from antique fairs and online. Everything comes back to the shop to be cleaned and restored. Then we sell the items in our shop or through our website. Our customers are homeowners or interior designers.

At the moment we are fitting out our new shop. Nearly everything in the shop is reclaimed. For example, the stairs (below) are made from wooden worktops taken from a school science laboratory!

Adam Hill
Reclamation dealer
Retrouvius Reclamation and Design
London, UK

Cast iron lion heads and a sign from the London underground railroad (which could be used to make an unusual tabletop) are just two of the interesting items for sale at Retrouvius, Adam Hill's store.

DESIGNING AND CONSTRUCTING GREEN BUILDINGS

In the future, most new buildings will be greener. They will be designed so that they conserve water and are energy efficient. Designers will also aim to make new buildings carbon neutral—they will produce zero carbon emissions! In the meantime, we can make existing buildings more environmentally friendly by weatherizing and retrofitting them.

A solar panel installer fits photovoltaic solar panels on the roof of a large store in New Jersey. The store estimates that it will reduce its main electricity usage by 25 percent by using solar power.

Weatherizing Our Homes

Weatherizing means adding new green modifications to old buildings to save energy and water. For example, insulation material can be installed to keep heat from escaping. This means less energy will be needed to keep a house warm.

These changes are good for the environment, and they save home owners and renters money, too. Making these modifications to homes is a big growth area for many home-improvement businesses—one that is creating a lot of new green jobs.

MAKING EXISTING HOMES GREENER

• Solar power (the power of the Sun) is a renewable energy source. A house can be designed with solar panels on the roof, or the panels can be retrofitted to existing houses or apartment buildings. Solar panels collect the Sun's power and use it in two ways. Solar thermal systems direct water through the solar panel. The water in the panel is heated by solar energy and then stored in a hot water tank for use around the house. Solar photovoltaic panels use special cells that react with sunlight to create electricity. The electricity can be used in the house, and if surplus energy is produced, it can be sold to a power company for use elsewhere.

• Many homes lose lots of heat through gaps around windows and doors. Weatherization workers check for gaps and fill them with special tape or foam that sets hard and plugs the leaks.

• Energy-efficiency technicians check heating, air-conditioning, and hot water systems to make sure they are working efficiently. Old, inefficient machines can be upgraded or replaced to save energy.

• Fitting insulation material in attics and walls keeps heat from escaping during the winter and keeps heat out in the summer. This cuts down the amount of energy used on heating and air-conditioning.

Here (right), a contractor fits eco-friendly insulation material in the loft of a house. The sheets of insulation material are made from renewable, chemical-free sheep's wool.

DESIGNING SUSTAINABLE LIVING: GREEN ARCHITECT

I first thought I might want to be an architect when I was 14, and someone suggested it to me during art classes. The idea just stuck.

My favorite projects to date have been the publicly funded "self build" houses I've worked on. These projects allow the end users to take part in planning and building their own homes. They can personalize the layouts, spaces, and colors of their homes as they build them.

The inspiration behind starting my green architectural practice was a desire to build small in a way that was new and interesting and needed exploring—and to keep the fun in architecture. Now I combine this work with part-time work for a bigger architecture firm.

Clients normally find me via my Web site. I talk with them and get to know what they are looking for. Then I work up ideas for the project and negotiate a price with the client. My ideas are then developed into client-approved designs, and I submit detailed technical plans to the local planning department.

What do I do in an average day? Well, last Friday I contacted the planners about one of my projects and we figured out some changes on my plans. Then I updated my client and created a new set of drawings. Then, I met another client and we visited a local joinery (carpentry) company to discuss the project's window frames and doors. The client is using trees from his own farm to cut down on CO2 emissions and using a local company to stimulate the local economy.

Robin Hillier
Architect and Company Director
Forever Green
Tunbridge Wells, Kent, UK

Designing New Green Buildings

Every new green house or apartment block will begin its life as an idea in the mind of a designer called an architect. Architects design houses, schools, sports stadiums, shopping malls—in fact, every building or structure you see around you has started out in an architect's imagination.

Designing a building takes technical know-how—the knowledge of how a building is constructed—and lots of creativity to make the building look good. Architects draw detailed plans of their designs by hand and use computer design programs. It takes several years at college or architect school to learn everything there is to know about designing buildings.

Many architecture companies are now specializing in designing green buildings. They think about how to make a building blend into the natural environment around it and how it will affect wild habitats and local wildlife. They include natural, renewable materials in their design. Sometimes they will create a design that uses parts of an old, existing building. These companies will want to employ creative, green-thinking new architects in the future.

It's All About Teamwork

It takes a big team of people doing many different jobs to make an architect's ideas come to life.

An architect normally works for a client (customer). The client will give the architect a brief for the new building. A brief is a "shopping list" of wants and needs that tells the architect what the building will be used for, how it should look, and how much it should cost. Here, an architect discusses her plans with her clients.

"In architecture, everyone carves out their own career route. Architects are a fairly anarchic bunch (freethinkers) so there is no saying where someone would end up. But one thing is for sure—zero carbon buildings will be mainstream by 2015. Eco-architecture will always be a challenge to the mainstream, as it demonstrates alternative ways of doing things, maybe less industrial, more thoughtful, maybe even poetic."

Robin Hillier,
Architect, Forever Green

Architects draw up plans of their designs, which are submitted to the local planning department for approval. The planners and other local residents will review the plans to be sure the design is acceptable for the area. Sometimes architects build models of their designs to show their clients or planners.

All of these jobs have been around for many years, but today people are looking for ways to do them in a more environmentally friendly way. Here are a few of the different roles involved in constructing a new building.

Structural Design Engineer. A structural design engineer is responsible for designing the structure of a building and bringing the architect's vision to life—all while working to local building codes and rules. A building must withstand local conditions, such as extreme weather or earth movements. The design must be strong and safe, so it cannot bend, twist, or collapse. A green structural engineer designs the building's structure to use as many renewable, eco-friendly materials as possible and to reduce the amount of wasted materials. Structural engineers advise the construction workers and inspect their work. They use mathematics and computer design programs.

Project Manager. A project manager (also known as the PM) works for a client—the person who is paying for the building. The client might be someone who is building his or her dream home or a large company that is building a development of hundreds of houses. It's the PM's job to look after every aspect of the project and make sure everything runs smoothly. A green project manager employs construction workers who use green methods. The PM also tracks down eco-friendly materials and finds ways to reduce, reuse, and recycle on the construction site.

The large windows on this house mean that it uses natural daylight instead of electric lights.

Buildings designed to use passive solar energy can be constructed from materials, such as adobe clay, that store heat and then slowly release it back into the house as the temperature outside drops.

GREEN DESIGN IDEAS

Here are just some of the design ideas that green architects use in their buildings:

• "Daylighting design" is a way to let lots of natural light into a building. The architect uses cleverly positioned windows, skylights, open courtyard areas, and glass roofing sections to light the building. Electric lights are not needed during the day. Natural sunlight is very good for the health of the people inside the building.

• Passive solar design aims to use the heat of the Sun to supply 100 percent of a building's heating needs. The position of the house in relation to the Sun's path throughout the day is figured out by the architect. The shape, size, and position of the windows are planned so that they let in heat at the hottest, sunniest times of the day.

• Buildings in especially hot places can be designed to stay cool without the use of air conditioning. For example, windows that face east and west and catch most of the Sun's heat are designed to be smaller than usual. Ceilings within the building are very high so that heat rises away from the living or working spaces.

• A home can be designed with a wind turbine in the backyard or garden or even on the roof. The turbine generates energy for the house and surplus power can be sold to a power company.

• Green architects understand that seeing nature is good for the people inside a building. Incorporating a view of a tree, or plants and grass, is important in green design.

• The "footprint" of a house is the amount of land it covers. In many towns and cities, space is now limited so homes with a small footprint are important. Architects think about how to build up or down to make the best use of space. Perhaps a building could have an underground garage or a rooftop garden.

Trees are often cut to make space for construction. Some green homes have been designed to incorporate existing trees into a new design. "Three Trees," by architect Jeremy Levine, is named after the three trees the house is built around.

The PM will also choose craftspeople and materials that are locally available to help support local jobs and communities. A PM must be organized, a good planner, and good at thinking ahead.

Carpenter. A carpenter works with wood—preparing and constructing wooden frames for buildings, making and fitting doors and window frames, building staircases, and making cupboards. A carpenter must know about all the different types of wood available. It's a practical job, but a good carpenter is also creative.

Plumber. Plumbers work with everything to do with water. They connect buildings to the local water supply and sewage system and install tubs, toilets, showers, and sinks. They also install heating equipment. Many plumbers design a complete water and heating system for a new building. Green plumbers figure out ways to conserve water and produce heat and hot water using the latest green technology, such as solar panels. The work of a plumber includes lots of practical work on construction sites, but it can also involve design work using computer programs.

> "The green-building community is at the cutting edge of an economic transformation that is going to save the world and humanity from our biggest mistakes."
>
> Van Jones, Special adviser on green jobs to the Obama administration

Near right: A project manager must ensure that a project is finished on time and within budget. The budget is the amount of money that a client wants to spend.

Far right: A project manager attends a site meeting with her client and the head of the construction crew.

Equipment can be installed in a house to clean the water so it can be reused for watering the garden and flushing the toilet.

Saving Energy in a New Green Home

New green homes can be designed to need less lighting and heating and to use green energy sources such as solar and wind power. Choosing energy-efficient appliances can save water and electricity, too. An energy-efficient refrigerator can use five times less energy than a standard one.

ECO-PAINT—ANY COLOR, AS LONG AS IT'S GREEN!

The paints we use to brighten our walls are usually made from non-renewable materials and highly toxic chemicals. Metals, such as lead, cadmium, and chromium, are sometimes used to give paints their colors. Petrochemicals, which give off greenhouse gases, are used as "binders" (to hold the paint together) and "carriers" (to allow it to spread). Paints made from chemicals give off harmful gases not just when they are wet but for many years after they have been applied to our walls. The gases they emit not only are bad for the environment, but can also cause health problems such as asthma, headaches, allergies, and even cancer.

Eco-friendly paint manufacturers are developing new paints that are good for the environment and good for our health. The manufacturers of eco-paint use plant dyes and natural minerals to give their paints color. They also use natural ingredients, such as water, oils made from plants, chalk, clay, and even milk, as binders and carriers. These paints do not give off harmful gases and are made from renewable substances. If the paints need to be thrown away, they are 100 percent biodegradable. They will rot away in landfills or even on a compost heap in your garden!

GREEN INSULATION

A well-insulated building uses less energy for heating and air conditioning. Many traditional insulation products are made from mixtures of chemicals and non-renewable petroleum substances, however. Green construction companies use natural insulation products made from renewable, biodegradable materials:

• Cellulose is an insulation material that is made from recycled paper and newspapers. Paper is biodegradable, but if it ends up in a landfill, it gives off methane as it decomposes, or rots away. Methane is a harmful greenhouse gas, so cellulose is a very eco-friendly type of insulation.

• Wood fiber insulation is made from wood chips compressed into thick boards. The wood chips are a byproduct of the lumber industry.

• Cotton insulation is made from leftover cotton and denim fiber. The fiber is collected from factories that make denim fabric for jeans and other clothing. The fiber is recycled into thick sheets of insulation material.

An added bonus of many natural insulation materials is that they are the byproduct of another industry, such as the cotton insulation shown here. This insulation is made of the same cotton product—denim—that is used to make jeans. This is a good way to reduce waste!

Burning wood on an open fire or in a wood burner is another good way to generate heat. The burning of wood produces carbon emissions, but trees naturally absorb carbon from the atmosphere. Therefore if we burn wood from forests that are being replanted, this source of heat can actually become carbon neutral.

Green Interior Design

So, your new home or office is carbon neutral. It is bright, warm—or cool—and energy efficient. The walls are decorated with chemical-free paints or wallpaper made from FSC (Forest Stewardship Council) certified paper. The floors are covered with reclaimed wood and bamboo.

Now you need some eco-friendly furniture and art to make your green home look beautiful!

Worldwide, artists and designers are creating amazing pieces of furniture and art in an environmentally friendly way. Some artists work with discarded materials they find on the street or in dumpsters. Others use recycled materials, such as glass, paper, and plastic bottles. If you think you would enjoy woodwork and metalwork, maybe you could learn to become a green furniture designer. If you have an artistic side to you, you could take art classes and consider becoming a professional artist who makes a living selling works of art.

Tom Deininger is an artist who creates found art—art made from things he finds that other people have thrown away. Tom finds his materials—including those used to create this self-portrait—in dumpsters and on the streets. His self-portrait is about the size of a door in an average room.

DESIGNS FOR GREENER LIVES: ECO-FRIENDLY INTERIOR DESIGNER

As a child, I was always drawing or painting. When I was nine years old, I made a little wooden model of a house with furniture that I could rearrange!

Once I got to the point of choosing a major on which to focus in school, interior design made perfect sense to me because it combines aspects of creativity and business.

I work on things such as researching and selecting environmentally friendly, sustainable wall materials, tiles, floor finishes, plumbing and lighting fittings, and cabinetry designs. I plan where to place furniture based on a client's needs, the scale of their home or available space, and the flow of traffic.

I correspond with suppliers on material pricing and availability. I meet with clients, architects, and contractors in the office and on-site. The best thing about my job is working with like-minded individuals who are passionate about design and life in general.

My dream project would be to design a water feature for the main lobby of a boutique hotel. Imagine a glass wall structure of curved lines with water cascading down the panels of glass. The water would actually be part of a hydroelectric system, where the energy of the flowing water would power electricity for the entire hotel!

Rachael Morton
Interior designer
Associates III
Denver, Colorado

Many artists and designers start their businesses straight out of art school. They set up Web sites to show off their work. They ask art and furniture galleries to display their work, or they send information and photographs of their work to interior designers.

Interior designers are creative people who design a building's inside spaces. They help their clients choose colors, flooring, furniture, fabrics—in fact, they create a complete "look" for a room or building. If you love colors, enjoy art and style magazines, and like to shop, interior design could be a career worth considering.

One job for interior designers is to choose fabrics for curtains and furniture. Sometimes they will design a unique piece of furniture that suits their client's style or the available space in a room.

INTERIOR STYLE AND THE THREE Rs

Green artists and designers produce their stylish creations while reusing junk, recycling trash, and saving raw materials and energy.

Oil Drum Chair/ Shopping Cart Chair

The people at VAHO in Barcelona, Spain, are designers and super recyclers! They use advertising canvasses (the type you might see strung across a street) to create unique pieces of furniture. Here an oil drum and a shopping cart have been made into chairs with covers and cushions made from old canvasses.

Miyake Wall

Japanese designer Arihiro Miyake has designed this innovative system that allows the easy building of partition walls. The wall sections are made from recycled plastic bottles and held together by magnets.

Garbage Cube

New York City artist Justin Gignac sells the city's garbage! Displayed in cubes, individual collections of trash picked from New York's streets can now be found on bookshelves and desks around the world.

"Environmentally friendly interior design just makes sense. It is possible to create absolutely gorgeous, luxurious spaces while preserving and even improving the condition of the earth. In the future I would like to see environmentally friendly, sustainable design become the industry standard."

Rachael Morton
Interior designer

GREEN OUTDOOR PLACES

Outside spaces are VERY important! Looking at trees and plants makes us feel good. Spending time outdoors in the fresh air has been proven by scientists to be good for our health. Working in a garden—digging, raking up leaves, carrying cans of water—is good exercise.

Good For People, Wildlife, and Cities

Trees and plants help cool the air in hot cities and naturally remove harmful carbon dioxide from the atmosphere. Spaces filled with plants and water, such as gardens and ponds, are important habitats for birds, insects, and other animals.

Above: Take a walk along a tree-lined street, watch some waterfowl on a city pond, or chill out on a park bench. Enjoying nature can be good for our health and put us in a good mood!

Any outside space is a vital part of the local environment whether it is a park, a small-town garden, a roof garden, or even a balcony. Many people do not have their own garden, so they are forming neighborhood groups to turn unused pieces of land in cities into community gardens.

Any green space around us is a good thing. If we can make that space more environmentally friendly, it becomes a very good thing!

COMMUNITY GARDENS

A community garden is a place created by, cared for, and used by the local people in a town or part of a city. Everyone who works in the garden does it for free and for the fun of it! Community gardens are used to grow flowers and healthy organic food for the gardeners to share or sell. They are also a great place for people who don't have a garden in which they can relax or get gardening exercise. Community gardens can teach young children about nature, and they bring together people of all ages and people from different cultures. These people may not have met or spoken to each other if it wasn't for the garden.

Above: Volunteers harvest produce from a community garden. The produce will be distributed to local people as part of a food bank program. Food banks are run by organizations who distribute food to individuals and families who cannot afford to buy food.

Left: Two garden designers create a garden on the roof of a city apartment building.

GROWING GREEN CITIES: MANAGING COMMUNITY GARDENS

My core role is to oversee the community gardens run by Greenest City and to manage the activities that take place in the gardens.

I spend about half my day on the computer answering emails and planning the children's program, youth drop-in, workshops, and English as a second language drop-in. I also spend a few hours a week in various meetings. And the rest of the time is spent outside in the garden!

This year we began a garden drop-in for youth. This program has been exceptionally popular with 20–25 hard-working young people coming along every week. At our second drop-in, I taught 20 attentive volunteers how to plant lettuce and kale seeds. The act of teaching young people how to plant their own food was inspiring.

Urban agriculture is good for the environment, the food is healthier, and it makes cities more beautiful. Growing food feeds us spiritually and emotionally. This is what motivates me to ensure that growing food in cities will continue and grow in the coming years.

Marilyn Brownlee
Urban Agriculture Manager
Greenest City Environmental Organization
Toronto, Ontario, Canada

Green Garden Materials

Without a doubt, grass is green—but in a world in which we need to conserve water, is grass actually "green?" Billions of gallons of precious water are used every year to keep the grass in gardens green and healthy.

Grass is a great landscaping material if you live in a cool climate with plenty of rain. It's natural, renewable, and a great habitat for millions of microscopic creatures. If you live in a hot, dry climate, however, a greener alternative would be a landscaping material such as gravel. Of course, garden stone needs to be quarried and transported, which has an impact on the environment, but the trade-off is that your garden will not need vast amounts of water to keep it looking beautiful.

Just as we do in our homes, we need to think about our garden's carbon footprint and balance all the different options to come up with the greenest solutions. We can choose locally available stone. We can buy wood for outdoor projects that is FSC (Forest Stewardship Council) approved. We can even use old materials, such as bricks and tiles, from reclamation yards.

Choosing the Right Plants

When Mother Nature was designing her "garden" she put particular species of plants in places where the climate was just right for them. Today, we like to experiment and choose plants from all over the world for our outdoor spaces. This doesn't always make good green sense, however. If your garden is in a hot, dry region, you will need to use gallons of water to keep alive a plant that was designed by nature to live in a damp, steamy rain forest. Green gardeners choose plants that are suited to the climate of their garden or that are native to that region.

As temperatures around the world gradually rise, it makes good green sense for all gardeners to choose plants that thrive in hot, dry conditions.

TIRES, CDs, AND OLD BOTTLES IN THE GARDEN?

Many innovative garden material companies are now using recycled materials to make garden coverings. Gravel-like, colorful glass chips are made from recycled bottles. Old CDs and DVDs can be crushed to make a sparkly garden covering, while used tires are turned into rubber gravel. Crushed sea shells—a byproduct from the shellfish food industry—are an eco-friendly, natural, and renewable way to cover garden surfaces.

This art installation was created by Spanish artist Marta Roman to highlight recycling on World Environment Day in 2005. The recycled car "plant container" is filled with cacti and other plants that do not require a lot of water to survive.

Above: This colorful garden gravel has been made from recycled tires.

ECO-FRIENDLY GARDEN IDEAS

• Use large tubs, barrels, or even old bathtubs to collect rainwater for plants. These can be linked to a simple system of pipes to collect water from a roof.

• Install garden lights that use solar power.

• Mulch the flower beds. This means covering the soil so it holds water and does not dry out. Mulches can be made from gravel, recycled glass, tree bark chips (a byproduct of the lumber industry), and compost.

• Make compost! Garden waste, lawn clippings, leaves, vegetable peelings, and other kitchen waste such as egg shells and teabags can all be put into a big pile in the garden and allowed to rot down to make new crumbly soil, or compost.

• Create a wild area—perhaps a patch of wild flowers, or a stack of old logs. This will quickly become a habitat for insects and small animals such as mice and toads.

Compost, like that made up of the organic scraps shown here, can be sprinkled on flower beds to feed the plants—no need for chemical fertilizers—and to keep the soil moist.

We can recycle old junk to make funky plant containers—for example, old chimney pots, wheelbarrows, metal buckets or large oil cans, bathtubs, and even old toilets and leather gardening boots! This plant display uses an old wooden crate and the base of an antique sewing machine—both items were found in dumpsters!

Creating Nature Gardens

Today, many people realize that it's important to care about nature and biodiversity. Biodiversity is short for "biological diversity." It means every living thing on Earth—every microorganism, plant, insect, animal, and person. We need to remember that Mother Nature designed things the way they are for a reason—to keep our planet healthy.

Each living thing has an impact on the other, and the "picture" of our natural world fits together like a jigsaw puzzle. When we cut down trees to build cities, or cover green spaces with concrete, we destroy plant life and wildlife habitats. This in turn affects biodiversity in an area. Gardens are a way that we can give back to nature and create habitats for animals.

By growing flowering plants we can give pollinator insects such as bees and butterflies pollen and nectar. These insects are vital to the health of our planet. Pollinators don't just pollinate garden plants. They also pollinate food crops and trees. Without bees we wouldn't be able to eat an apple or drink a cup of coffee!

Bushes and trees give birds a place to roost and build nests. Like insects, birds help pollinate plants. When they eat insects, they also help keep the natural balance of wildlife just right in a habitat. We can encourage birds to come into our gardens by building nest boxes and hanging up bird feeders.

This honeybee (left) is covered by pollen from apple blossom flowers. A garden water feature—whether it's as big as a pond or as small as a tiny ornamental fountain—gives birds a place to drink and bathe (center), and it can quickly become a habitat for insects, frogs, and newts. A red cardinal (right) enjoys a meal of seeds from a garden feeder.

PRESIDENT OBAMA'S VEGETABLE GARDEN

When Kitchen Gardeners International launched "Eat the View" in 2008, the campaign's number one target was the White House. As President Barack Obama's presidential campaign gained momentum, so did the "Eat the View" campaign to have a vegetable garden planted on the president's lawn. The campaign was even one of the nine winners of the "On Day One" contest—a competition to identify nine projects (nine for 2009) to be presented to the new administration on its first day in office. Just like President Obama's campaign, "Eat the View" was successful. The First Vegetable Garden is now in place. The garden's produce will be eaten at the White House and given away to homeless shelters in Washington, D.C.

"The last time food was grown on the White House lawn was in 1943, when the country was at war, the economy was struggling and people were looking to the First Family for leadership. It made sense before and it makes sense again as we try to live within our own means and those of the planet."

Roger Doiron, Kitchen Gardeners International

Gardens We Can Eat

If we are going to use the important resources of soil and water, why not use them to create an edible garden—a garden we can eat?

Kitchen Gardeners International is a network of over 10,000 gardeners in 100 countries. KGI helps individuals and communities learn how to grow their own healthy, sustainable produce. In 2008, KGI launched the "Eat the View" campaign. Many public buildings have large areas of unproductive lawn.

First Lady Michelle Obama works with kids from Washington's Bancroft Elementary School to break ground for a White House vegetable garden in spring 2009.

In towns and cities there are areas of unused land that are used only as a place for dumping garbage. The "Eat the View" campaign encourages people to identify spaces in their local area that could be used to grow food and then campaign to have them turned into an edible view!

Become a Garden Designer

Many people design and care for their own garden, while others employ a gardener to tend their outdoor space. Some people even use the services of a garden designer.

Just like an interior designer, garden designers take an outdoor space and give it a completely new "look." They select the hard landscaping (items such as paving, walls, or decking) and choose the plants. Garden design is a very creative career. A designer's clients may want you to turn a tiny yard squeezed between city apartment buildings into a place where they can grow vegetables and entertain friends.

COMPOST TOILETS

Removing sewage waste is a big problem in our modern world. Trillions of gallons of water are needed to flush toilets. Sewage sludge (what's left after sewage has been treated and the water recycled) needs a place to go. That place is often a landfill. Sewage can escape and cause pollution to rivers and groundwater. Often raw sewage is pumped into the oceans. Imagine if we all dealt with our own sewage and used it to feed the plants in our gardens or backyards.

OK. You might actually NOT want to imagine that, but this is exactly what composting toilets do. There are many different designs and systems, but the general idea is always the same. The toilet looks the same as a normal toilet, but the waste is stored in a container where it is "broken down" by microorganisms and turned into fertile compost that can be put straight onto the garden. Compost toilets are hygienic and non-smelly, and they can turn a substance that is unpleasant and inconvenient but also renewable into something very useful!

Think about it....

Vegetables and fruit look as colorful and beautiful as flowers and shrubs, and they still provide a haven for wildlife. This little garden has been created using a mixture of vegetables and herbs.

They might want the designer to design and build a lake or even create a garden with a theme, such as an English cottage garden or a Buddhist temple garden.

Designing gardens involves having a good knowledge of plants and construction. The work includes thinking up your own ideas and working closely with clients to bring their ideas alive.

Garden design and horticulture (the science and art of growing plants) can be studied at college, at night school classes, or even by taking online courses. Many gardeners also start out as apprentices or general laborers for a garden design company.

As more and more people want to live in an eco-friendly way, green garden design is becoming important. Offering clients a service designing sustainable, environmentally friendly gardens, or a service caring for their garden in an eco-friendly way, is a growth area for the future.

CAREER PROFILE

SUSTAINABLE, ECO-FRIENDLY GARDENS: GREEN GARDENER

After school I got a job in a flower shop and I did some volunteering in one of the many historic gardens in this part of the country. The work was mostly things like emptying litter bins (trash containers) and painting benches, but I loved talking to the "real" gardeners. I decided to take an online course in garden design and one in horticulture. Then I started offering my gardening services—putting leaflets through the doors of houses with big gardens! At home we'd always been pretty "green" so I wanted to offer an eco-friendly service.

I mow lawns using a manual push mower that uses no electricity or petrol (gasoline), and I weed flower beds and clean out ponds. All the grass clippings and cuttings go on my compost heap to make compost for use on my clients' gardens.

The best times are when a client asks me to work on a specifically green project. I designed and built an organic vegetable garden for one family. We used reclaimed wooden floorboards to create edges for the vegetable beds. I sourced all the organic seeds online, and I even went to our local stables to get some sacks of horse manure to feed the soil!

I don't think I'm going to get rich, but I love my work, and it keeps me really fit!

Ellen Dalton
Eco-friendly gardener
Greenfingers
Penzance, Cornwall, UK

Garden designers combine design work using computer programs and drawing by hand (facing page) with a lot of time spent outside doing physical tasks such as planting, mowing lawns, building walls, and digging ponds.

CHAPTER 5

GREEN CITIES OF THE FUTURE

It has been estimated that in the United States 89 million new homes will need to be built in the next 40 years. If we think about what those homes and new communities will need—schools, transportation systems, water, energy sources, places to work, places to shop and enjoy leisure time—and then consider all that we've already talked about in this book, it all adds up to just one thing—the need to build eco-cities.

A green city shouldn't just be a good place to live now, but also hundreds of years from now—that's the essence of sustainability. Dockside Green is a sustainable development planned for Victoria, British Columbia, Canada. Residents will live in green homes surrounded by trees, open green spaces, waterways, and bike and walking trails.

Where Should We Build?

It's an exciting time to be involved in the planning of new towns and cities. The need to stop climate change and care more for our environment means urban planners, architects, and others involved in city design are thinking creatively about how we can live in new ways.

Where we build our cities is an important thing to consider. We need to protect wild habitats, such as forests, wherever possible. People like to live near water, but building close to rivers might be dangerous if climate change causes weather that makes rivers flood. Brownfield sites are a good option for new developments. These sites were previously used for industry and are often contaminated with waste.

Turning disused, polluted brownfield sites into flourishing, clean eco-cities is a good use of space in areas where land available for building is limited.

CAREERS IN DEVELOPING NEW CITIES

Environmental Engineers
Environmental engineers deal with environmental issues such as air pollution control or waste disposal and recycling. They might also be involved with designing water supply or waste removal systems. In the planning of a new city, environmental engineers might analyze the impact of the new city on wildlife and wild habitats. They will consider how much pollution and what level of carbon emissions the new city will produce. An environmental engineer might work for the local government. Others might work for private companies involved in the developments of new buildings, or even whole cities.

Urban Planners
This career involves planning towns and cities and making the best use of the available land to give a community everything it needs. Planners also approve or adapt plans put forward by construction companies or developers. Most planners work for local governments.

Planners need to examine data: How many people will walk or drive to a new school? How much water will be used in a new housing development? They also talk to local people at planning meetings and balance different opinions: For example, a new industrial complex will create jobs, but an area of countryside will be destroyed.

Planning will be at the heart of creating eco-cities. The planner must incorporate railways, wind farms, and work places within walking distance of homes—planning a city and incorporating all these factors will be an exciting and challenging career.

BEAUTIFUL, PRODUCTIVE ROOFTOPS: GREEN ROOF DESIGNER

I actually stumbled upon my career while working for an organization that builds urban agriculture projects, the Environmental Youth Alliance in Vancouver. When a local businessman asked our organization to help him build a green roof and rooftop vegetable garden, I jumped at the chance to learn how. I took two courses on green roof design at the British Columbia Institute of Technology and read many books on the subject.

I spend a quarter of my time designing, using either computer programs, or doing hand drawings and another quarter of my week online or on the phone sourcing recycled or environmentally friendly materials for my projects. The rest of my week is spent building green roofs and rooftop gardens, which involves getting really dirty and using power tools. It's great to be able to design and build, because I get to see ideas through to completion.

My favorite project so far was my very first green roof. It was on the warehouse roof of an environmentally friendly office supplies company in Vancouver's Downtown Eastside. The green roof has brought bees and other wildlife into the downtown core.

Erika Richmond
Green Roof Designer
Erika Richmond Green Roof Design
Vancouver, British Columbia, Canada

A self-sufficient, low-energy city will need space to build wind farms to supply energy. It will also need places to build reservoirs for water and ways to dispose of its garbage.

How Will We Live?

In a new eco-city all the homes and other buildings will be built using green materials and the construction methods we've already looked at in this book. There might even be a plan to use only construction materials that can be found locally. Sherford is a future green community under construction in the United Kingdom. The town will be home to 12,000 people. Every home in Sherford will be built using sustainable materials that can be sourced within 50 miles (80 kilometers) of the town.

Eco-cities will be smaller than many of the cities built in the past. Smaller cities will allow for homes, shops, schools, medical centers, and other "everyday" places to be in close proximity to each other so people can easily walk to them.

TREASURE ISLAND

Treasure Island is a manmade island off the coast of San Francisco. A plan is underway to turn the island into a virtually self-sufficient city for 13,500 residents. A wind farm and solar panels on buildings will supply the city's energy. Fresh produce will be supplied by a 20-acre (8-hectare) organic farm within walking distance of the city's center.

A green roof planted with sedum plants

Eco-cities will include many green public spaces. They might even include places where food can be grown. Imagine how much fuel would be saved if all the fruits and vegetables that people in a city needed to buy were fresh and available just a short walk or cycle ride from their homes.

How Will We Move Around the City?

In eco-cities, priority will be given to walkers and cyclists over car users. Pedestrian walkways and bicycleways will crisscross the city, and the city center will be within walking distance of every home. In the new eco-town of Sherford, each new house comes with a free bicycle!

DRAGONFLY

Architect Vincent Callebaut's "Dragonfly" is a revolutionary project that explores how people can live, work, and grow the food they need in urban environments where space is limited. Two towers of housing and offices are surrounded by gardens and public agriculture and leisure spaces. The Dragonfly's "wings" would be a kind of vertical farm housing orchards, vegetable gardens, rice fields, and pasture for animals.

Dragonfly, designed to be built along the East River in New York City, is a perfect example of an architect's creativity and skills being put to use to create a green future.

GREEN WALLS

Buildings in some places are using their walls to bring plants and nature into cities. Madrid's CaixaForum museum (below) has a 79-foot-high (24-meter-high) wall on the front of the building made up of 15,000 plants from 250 different plant species. The Vancouver Aquarium has a wall covered with plastic modules (containers) that are filled with wildflowers, ferns, and low-growing plants.

A network of trains or buses running on green electricity will connect every place in an eco-city. The city might even have a fleet of electric cars that are free for any resident to use.

How Will We Power the City?

The eco-city of the future will be designed to generate all the energy it needs using solar panels on the buildings and other green energy sources. The city might have its own wind farm or hydroelectric power plant built on the city's reservoir. Cities located near the coast might even obtain all their electricity from tidal power.

It's not just eco-cities that will use these sources of power in the future. With fossil fuels running out and carbon emissions damaging our planet, governments worldwide are looking to generate more of a nation's energy from alternative energy sources. This is a big growth area for green jobs. Wind farms and other green power plants need engineers to design, test, build, and install the equipment. The power plants must also be maintained and operated.

GREEN ENERGY SOURCES

• Bio-energy is the use of renewable plants, such as oilseed rape plants, wheat, and grasses, to make energy. The plant matter can be turned into liquid fuel or burned to create energy. The plant matter can also be rotted down in a process called anaerobic digestion to produce a gas that can be used as an energy source. Bio-gas can also be created from animal manure, food waste, and sewage.

• Hydroelectric power is generated by moving water. A power plant and a dam are built on a large river. The dam stops the flow of water and collects it in a giant reservoir. The water is then released from the reservoir—to continue on its way along the river—in a controlled way. As the water is released, it rushes through a "gateway" of huge turbine blades (left, above). The power of the water turns the blades, which generates electricity in the power plant.

• Tidal power is created using the in and out movement of the ocean's tides (or tides in large lakes). The movement of the water powers turbines to generate electricity.

• Geothermal power uses heat from under the ground. The heat comes from volcanic activity, from solar energy stored in the ground, and from heat generated naturally in the soil. Pipes filled with a liquid are run underground. The liquid is warmed by the geothermal heat, and the heat is then extracted from the liquid using a heat pump. Systems can be installed to power a single home or many buildings.

In London, drivers pay a "congestion charge" of around $12.00 to enter the city center. This scheme was designed to encourage people to use public transportation instead of their cars. Electric, hybrid (electric and gas), and other eco-friendly cars do not have to pay the charge. Schemes like this can reduce carbon emissions in cities. The picture above shows an electric car recharging its battery in a parking spot in London.

GREEN ENERGY CAREERS

There are many exciting job opportunities available in the creation of green energy. Skilled green energy workers will be in demand for many years to come.

WIND TURBINE ENGINEER

Wind energy engineers, or windsmiths, are trained to assemble, maintain, and repair wind turbines. Being comfortable with heights is an important requirement for this job—you might be working 300 feet (90 m) above the ground, or high in the air above the ocean if you are repairing an offshore turbine!

WIND ANALYST

You can't just build a wind farm anywhere. Finding the best place to build a wind farm is the job of a wind analyst. When a potential site has been identified, the wind analyst needs to figure out how much electricity will be generated by the wind farm. The analysis team sets up masts with equipment that records how strong the wind blows and in which direction. They analyze the results, sometimes for up to five years, and recommend whether the site will be a good place to build wind turbines.

WAVE POWER ENGINEER

Wave power engineers are at the cutting edge of a new, fast-growing technology. They use computers to design the equipment that harnesses the ocean's power. Powerful waves are needed to generate electricity, so the equipment must be able to withstand ocean storms and not be swept away! Wave power engineers build the equipment, test it in a wave tank (like a large swimming pool), and then install it out at sea. With such a new technology there are engineering problems to solve every day.

How Will We Dispose of the City's Waste?

Recycling will be an important part of living in an eco-city. Landfills require vast areas of space, so eco-cities will aim to recycle or reuse all their waste. This is good for the environment and also good for the community—studies have shown that recycling creates six times as many jobs as operating landfill systems.

A city's food and garden waste can be turned into compost for use on farms or in gardens. Items that are still useful will be cleaned, overhauled, and resold. All other waste will be sorted, processed, and recycled.

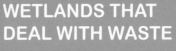

WETLANDS THAT DEAL WITH WASTE

All of the sewage waste that a city produces can actually be treated using specially built wetlands. Sewage can be filtered through fields of reeds and plants such as rushes, lilies, and water hyacinths. These plants naturally filter the sewage, break down the waste, and absorb harmful toxins. Bacteria, fungi, fish, and snails in the wetland can also help with this process. The wetlands need no energy to run, create a wildlife habitat, and produce an end product of clean water.

These photos (top and center left) show a sewage-treatment wetland when it was first built and the lush wetland two years later.

RECYCLED ART

At the Norcal Recycling and Transfer Station in San Francisco, the garbage facility runs an Artist-in-Residence program. Local artists are given a work space at the station and are allowed access to all the waste material. The artists create artwork using everything from scrap wood and metal to leftover house paint. Large pieces of sculpture are on display in a 3-acre (1.2-ha) sculpture garden that provides a green buffer between the waste plant and local homes. (See page 62 for the Web sites showing the artists' work.)

Above: Artists worldwide are creating art from trash. This trash elephant by artist Anthony Heywood is entitled "Broken Family." It is on display at the Bondi "Sculptures By The Sea" exhibition in Australia.

CHAPTER 6

GREEN PLACES FOR WORK, LEARNING, AND FUN

The CIS Tower in Manchester, UK, is an office block that generates all its own power using solar panels (the blue panels in the photograph). The building generates 180,000 kWh of power per year—enough to supply all the energy needs of 73 homes.

Green design ideas and construction methods can be used in the construction of any building, from shops to factories, schools, or sports stadiums.

Eco-school

Howe Dell school in Hertfordshire, UK, is one of the greenest schools in the world. The school is heated using the world's first Inter-seasonal Heat Transfer (IHT) system. This innovative, computer-controlled system takes the heat from the sunshine that falls on the paved playground and stores it for heating the school in the winter. The IHT also reverses this process and stores cold winter air for cooling the school in the summer.

Solar panels supply the school's hot water and electricity, while skylights in the classrooms and corridors eliminate the need for electric light on bright days. Rainwater is collected to flush the toilets, and the school's desks are made from recycled drainpipes. The school's roof is made from low-growing sedum plants.

The green roof insulates the building and is used as a living classroom where the students can study biodiversity.

Building A Green Future

More and more parents want their children to learn in environmentally friendly schools. People want to work in green offices and factories, and they want to enjoy their leisure time and vacations in places that are caring for the planet. The future for green construction workers, green designers and gardeners, and those working in careers that help us save energy and resources is looking good. If construction is of interest to you, here are two great facts: There are thousands of opportunities each year to get started. A high percentage of workers in the construction industry eventually start their own companies and become their own bosses!

"For the first time in history, more than half the world's population lives in cities. We'll rebuild half the planet's buildings in the next 50 years... Now that modern technology has put us in a position that we can do anything, what will we do?"

Bruce Mau, Bruce Mau Design, Toronto

The Hearst Tower's "diagrid" (diagonal grid) design doesn't just look good but also gives the building its structural strength. The innovative design meant that the building could be constructed using approximately 2,000 tons less steel than a normal skyscraper of this size.

A GREEN SKYSCRAPER

The Hearst Tower was the first "green" building in New York. The skyscraper was completed in 2006 on the site of the original Hearst building, which still forms the new skyscraper's base. The building is made from four-story-high triangles of glass and steel—about 80 percent of the steel used was recycled. The tower's roof collects rainwater that is stored in a giant tank. The water is used in the building's air-conditioning system to irrigate trees and plants in the building and for the three-story-high glass "Icefall" water sculpture in the lobby. The sculpture helps keep the building's lobby cool. To save energy, motion sensors are placed in all the offices. The sensors switch off lights and computers when a room is vacant for a certain amount of time.

THE WORLD'S GREENEST HOLIDAY RESORT

AquaCity, a self-powered luxury resort in Slovakia, is often voted the world's greenest resort in tourism awards. All the energy to power the resort's hotels, water park, spa, and restaurants comes from geothermal power. Beneath the foothills of Slovakia's High Tatras mountains are vast underground lakes of naturally hot geothermal water. AquaCity draws hot water from the lakes, uses the heat to power the resort, and then returns the water back to the lakes. The resort's geothermal power is supplemented by solar power. Powering AquaCity in this way saves nearly 30 tons of carbon emissions every day!

So, do you remember that futuristic green home and city described on the opening pages of this book? The fact is that the advances in technology that can help us build green homes and cities are out there now. All the industry is waiting for is people like you!

The La Rosa campsite in Yorkshire, UK, may not be one of the most hi-tech vacation destinations, but it's certainly one of the greenest! Everything on the site has been recycled, reclaimed, or found—from the old caravans filled with funky, junky, knick-knacks to an open-air bathtub in the orchard. Campers use a compost toilet (housed in the caravan seen here), cook on open fires, and light their caravans or tents with candles or low-energy Christmas tree lights.

START YOUR GREEN FUTURE NOW...

It's exciting to have plans and dreams for the future. It's also exciting to try new things. Here are some fun projects to help you find out what you enjoy doing and to whet your appetite for your future career.

BE A GREEN INTERIOR DESIGNER...

If you like the idea of decorating and creating innovative, green interiors, get some experience in your own bedroom. (First make sure you check with the person who makes the rules in your house!) You don't have to re-do everything. Even small changes will make your space greener. If you can repaint the walls, buy natural paint or reuse leftover paints—try mixing different-colored leftovers to create a new color.

Visit local thrift shops to scout around for funky, second-hand furniture, lamps, and photo frames. An old pair of jeans can be cut into squares and made into a recycled cushion cover. Add some plants to the room to improve the "look" and air quality. Look online for more ideas.

MAKE SOME RECYCLED TRASH ART...

Have a trash art workshop day using your family's garbage and recycling. Keep a lookout for a couple of weeks for anything interesting that your family is throwing away—clothes, old shoes, food cartons and containers, magazines, and bottles. If something is clean and interesting, it doesn't matter what it once was—what it CAN be is all that's important now. Check out the garage. Does your family have any leftover house paint? Even old bottles of nail polish might be useful. Get some equipment together—scissors, a hot glue gun (these are inexpensive to buy—or you can borrow one), and craft tape. Invite some friends, make some snacks, and get creative! Try making a self-portrait sculpture or collage, or create a fantasy garbage animal.

VISIT A GREEN WORKPLACE

Organize a visit to a green workplace. You can go with family or friends or find out if your school will arrange a visit. Places to visit might include:
• a wind farm;
• a solar power farm;
• a hydroelectric plant;
• a recycling center;
• a community garden or city farm.
Look online for places in your area, and find out if they have visitor days.

THINK LIKE A GREEN ARCHITECT...

On your own or with a group of friends, imagine you are a green architect assessing your school for possible green improvements. You can produce a report on your findings, draw sketches of your ideas, or even create visuals by taking photographs and using Photoshop programs on your computer. Think about all the green design ideas in this book. How could your school save energy? Is there wasted space where plants and trees could grow, or even vegetables to create an "edible view"? What would make the building a nicer place to be? Your architect project can be completely practical or a vision of a green school for the future.

MAKE YOUR NEIGHBORHOOD A GREEN PLACE...

You may not be able to change the design of your neighborhood yet, but one thing we can all do is make sure our neighborhood is a clean place to be. Talk to neighbors and friends about starting a "Neighborhood Clean-up" group. Spending just one day a month picking up litter will make your area a greener place to be. For help getting started, go to:

http://planetgreen.discovery.com/work-connect/bold-green-neighborhood-cleanup.html

BE SMART, BE SAFE!

Please get permission from the adult who cares for you before making trips to new places or volunteering in your free time. Always let him or her know where you are going and who you are meeting.

GLOSSARY

architect A highly trained designer who conceives and designs buildings. Architects must be able to combine creative ideas with an understanding of the technical aspects of constructing a building

biodegradable Something that will decompose (rot away)

biodigester A device that is used to turn plant material, animal manure, or food waste into compost and energy sources. Biodigesters can be small enough for just one household or large enough to treat the waste of a whole town. Depending on the material put into the biodigester, bacteria inside breaks the waste down and can turn it into compost, liquid fertilizers (plant foods), or liquids that can be used as fuel. As the waste breaks down, it also releases methane gas. The gas is collected and can be used to heat water or produce electricity

biodiversity The shortened term for "biological diversity." It means the numbers of different species of living thing on Earth—microorganisms, animals, humans, and plants

carbon emissions The release of carbon dioxide, or CO_2, into the atmosphere as a result of burning fossils fuels such as coal and oil. The amount of CO_2 in Earth's atmosphere has been steadily increasing, contributing to climate change and causing harm to plant and animal life

carbon footprint The way in which we measure how much carbon dioxide, or CO_2, a person, a building, or a business is responsible for. For example, each time people go for a ride in a car or use electricity, their activities produce CO_2. The amount of CO_2 they are responsible for is their carbon footprint

carbon neutral Producing no carbon emissions. A building using only green energy may be carbon neutral

climate change A gradual warming of Earth's climate. It is caused by the burning of fossil fuels that give off greenhouse gases and trap too much of the Sun's heat in Earth's atmosphere

compost Organic material added to soil to improve its ability to support plant growth. Compost consists of decomposed materials such as plant matter, food waste, or manure. In a garden, materials for composting can be placed in a big pile. Over the course of several months, bacteria, microorganisms, and decomposing animals such as earthworms will break the waste down into a soil-like material that can be worked into the soil and used to feed plants

fossil fuels Fuels, such as oil, coal, and gas, that formed over the course of millions of years from the decaying remains of plants and animals

glaciers Large bodies of ice that move slowly down a slope or valley and spread outward on the land. Some glaciers move just a few inches or centimeters, each day, while others can move several feet or meters, in a day

greenhouse gases Gases created by the burning of fossil fuels. Carbon dioxide, nitrous oxide, and methane are all greenhouse gases. These gases are causing the Sun's heat to become trapped in Earth's atmosphere—just as the glass of a greenhouse traps heat—and are causing climate change

microorganisms Tiny living things—bacteria, fungi, animals, and plants—that are too small to see without the help of a microscope

organic In general, referring to a substance that is based on carbon, which includes all living material. In food production, "organic" refers to food produced entirely naturally and without chemicals

pollution Any substance that damages or poisons the air, water, or land. Chemicals spilled into a river, dust in the air from a construction project, or garbage left on a beach are all forms of pollution

renewable Something that will not run out, such as the Sun's energy or wind power; or something that can be replaced in a short amount of time, such as plants

sustainable Able to go on into the future. Sustainable construction is construction that uses renewable materials and does not damage the environment for future generations

wetland A natural habitat of rivers, ponds, lakes, and marshes. Wetlands are home to fish, water insects and animals, and waterfowl

FURTHER INFORMATION

www.greenforall.org/
Go to "Green For All" to find out about
Green–Collar Careers.

www.greenforall.org/resources/green-
    jobs-guidebook
Download this *Green Jobs Guidebook*, which
profiles over 200 green jobs with details about
the experience or qualifications needed.

www.treehugger.com/design_architecture/
    ?dcitc=th_nav
Treehugger is a Web site packed with green
ideas for every part of our lives. Check
out this link to see the latest and coolest
architectural and design innovations.

weburbanist.com/2008/05/26/cargo-
    container-homes-and-offices/
Here you can see recycled shipping
containers in use as homes and workplaces.

vincent.callebaut.org/projets-groupe-tout.html
Find out more about architect Vincent
Callebaut's visionary "Dragonfly" project
and see other examples of innovative
Callebaut projects.

www.oneplanetliving.org/index.html
One Planet Living is a campaign supported
by the WWF (World Wildlife Fund). The
campaign identifies ten important criteria
for a more sustainable future for the
whole world.

ecofaebrick.com/products.html
Visit this site to find out more about making
bricks from cow dung!

www.restoreonline.org/decon.htm
Visit the ReStore Home Improvement Center's
Web site and watch their deconstruction
team dismantle and reclaim buildings due
for demolition.

www.eattheview.org/
Read more about the "Eat the View"
campaign to turn unproductive spaces
into productive places to grow food.

www.eere.energy.gov/
www.ic.gc.ca/eic/site/mib-
dgif.nsf/eng/h_hu00001.html
Find out about renewable energy.

www.sunsetscavenger.com/AIR/
    artists.php?t=d
www.sunsetscavenger.com/AIR/
    sculpturegarden.php?t=d
View the artists' work at the Norcal Recycling
and Transfer Station in San Francisco and
see sculpture in the sculpture garden.

erikarichmonddesign.wordpress.com/
Follow Erika Richmond's work on green
rooftops (see career profile page 50) and
see some of her design projects.

INDEX

INDEX

ABOUT THE AUTHOR

Ruth Owen has worked in developing, editing, and writing children's books for more than ten years. She writes children's fiction under the name of Dee Phillips, but non-fiction books are her real passion. Ruth particularly enjoys working on books about animals and the natural world. In fact, the first book she can remember buying was when, at the age of six, she saved up to buy *Gorilla Baby*, a book from her school book club that told the story of Patty Cake, a gorilla that was born in the Central Park Zoo in New York. Ruth tries to be as eco-friendly as possible in her everyday life. She loves gardening and grows organic vegetables. Her garden is filled with interesting old junk rescued from landfills! The vegetables and plants receive regular doses of organic manure from Ruth's three pet llamas.

Printed in the USA—CG